GOING TO SCHOOL
DURING THE
CIVIL RIGHTS MOVEMENT

by Rachel A. Koestler

Consultant: Beverly M. Gordon, Associate Professor
Ohio State University, Columbus
Articles by Beverly M. Gordon have been published in *The Review of Educational Research, The Journal of Negro Education,* and *Racism and Racial Inequality.*

Blue Earth Books

an imprint of Capstone Press
Mankato, Minnesota

Blue Earth Books are published by Capstone Press
151 Good Counsel Drive, P.O. Box 669, Mankato, Minnesota 56002
http://www.capstone-press.com

Library of Congress Cataloging-in-Publication Data
Koestler, Rachel A., 1973–
    Going to school during the civil rights movement / by Rachel A. Koestler.
    p. cm.—(Going to school in history)
    Includes bibliographical references (p. 31) and index.
    ISBN 0-7368-0799-3
    1. Segregation in education—United States—History—20th century—Juvenile literature. 2. School integration—United States—History—20th century—Juvenile literature. 3. Civil rights movements—United States—History—20th century—Juvenile literature. [1. Segregation in education—History—20th century. 2. School integration—History—20th century. 3. Civil rights movements—History—20th century. 4. Education—History—20th century.] I. Title. II. Series.
LC214.2 .K64 2002
379.2'63'0973—dc21

                                  00-011626

Summary: Discusses the history of the Civil Rights movement and the social life of children during this time. Explores segregated school systems and conflicts during integration. Includes activities and sidebars.

Editorial Credits

Designer and Illustrator: Heather Kindseth
Product Planning Editor: Lois Wallentine
Photo Researchers: Heidi Schoof and Judy Winter

Photo Credits

Schomburg Center for Research in Black Culture, New York Public Library, cover; Library of Congress, 3 (all), 8 (left and middle), 11 (bottom), 13, 15, 17 (top), 18, 20, 27 (all); Archive Photos, 5, 8 (right); Bettmann/CORBIS, 6, 7, 12, 14, 23, 29 (top); Lambert/Archive Photos, 11 (top); Private Collection, 17 (bottom); Capstone Press/Gary Sundermeyer, 19 (all); CORBIS, 21; AP Wide World Photos, 24; Flip Schulke/CORBIS, 28, 29 (bottom)

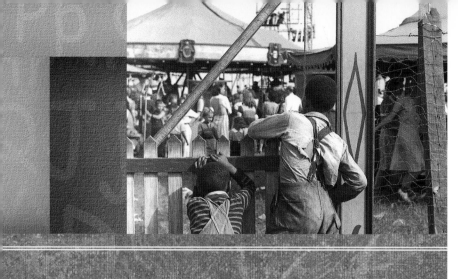

Contents

Struggle toward Equality

In the late 1600s, slave traders began kidnapping Africans and bringing them to North America as slaves. Slave traders sold most of these Africans to plantation owners. Plantation owners depended on the slaves to work in their large fields. In 1801, it became illegal for slave traders to bring new slaves to the United States. But plantation owners continued to buy and sell American-born Africans.

Slaves led difficult lives. Men, women, and children worked six days a week doing hard labor. Slave children began working around age 5 or 6. Some plantation owners harshly punished slaves who complained. Plantation owners often broke up slave families by selling some members to other plantations. Slaves lived in crude one- or two-room cabins in the plantation slave quarters.

Enslaved Africans wanted to be free. By the mid-1800s, slavery was illegal in many Northern U.S. states. Many slaves ran away from plantations and escaped to the North on the Underground Railroad. This system of safe houses and secret routes ran from Southern states to the North and Canada. Many people who opposed slavery took escaped slaves into their houses and hid them from slave catchers.

After the North defeated the South in the Civil War (1861–1865), all African Americans were free from slavery. But many whites still treated African Americans poorly. Many white Southerners were bitter about losing the war. They did not want African Americans getting an education and taking jobs that used to be only for whites. Throughout the South and in some parts of the North, city officials built separate bathrooms, restaurants, schools, shops, and theaters for African Americans. Many African Americans also lived in separate neighborhoods. These segregated areas often were rundown and poorly kept.

In 1909, a multiracial group of people founded the National Association for the Advancement of Colored People (NAACP). This organization was devoted to gaining and protecting equal rights for African Americans. In the 1950s, the NAACP began working for desegregation and equal rights. This struggle for equality was called the Civil Rights movement. Over time, this movement changed laws and affected life in the United States forever.

An African American girl leaves a restaurant through a door labeled "for colored." In 1896, the U.S. Supreme Court ruled that segregation was legal as long as equal services were provided.

FOR WHITE   FOR COLORED

Civil rights activists boycotted buses to protest segregation in public transportation.

People who worked in the Civil Rights movement were called civil rights activists. Civil rights activists were people of all races. Many civil rights activists participated in marches, boycotts, sit-ins, and voter registration drives, hoping to end segregation and change racial laws. These demonstrations attracted the attention of the U.S. government. Demonstrations were a peaceful way of showing the U.S. government that African Americans wanted equality. But during many demonstrations, police officers and local whites attacked civil rights activists. Police officers arrested and fined activists even though their demonstrations were peaceful.

In 1961, civil rights activists organized Freedom Rides in the eastern United States. People began these bus rides after the U.S. government outlawed segregation on public transportation. Freedom Riders were activists who rode from state to state on desegregated, or integrated, buses.

Much violence took place during the Civil Rights movement. Many African Americans and civil rights activists were killed in mob attacks and lynchings. Hate groups such as the Ku Klux Klan, or KKK, often used what they called the "lynch law" to justify killing civil rights activists and African Americans. If a person was accused of a crime, the mob believed they had the right to hang the accused without a fair trial. Mobs wrongfully accused most lynch victims. Mob members often went unpunished.

Many people participated in the Civil Rights movement. Together, civil rights activists made changes in government laws that they could not have made alone. These changes included school desegregation, the Civil Rights Act of 1957, the Voting Rights Act of 1965, and the establishment of citizenship schools.

Angry whites often attacked Freedom Riders at bus stations. The whites sometimes formed mobs and burned freedom buses.

7

Events during the Civil Rights Movement

Ruby Bridges becomes the first African American student to attend a desegregated elementary school in New Orleans, Louisiana.

David Richmond, Franklin McCain, Joseph McNeil, and Ezell Blair Jr. stage a sit-in at the F. W. Woolworth's store in Greensboro, North Carolina, when they are refused service. This incident inspired other sit-ins throughout the South.

More than 250,000 civil rights activists gather for the March on Washington, the largest civil rights demonstration in Washington, D.C.'s history.

In a series of cases called *Brown v. the Board of Education, Topeka*, the Supreme Court outlaws segregation in public schools.

Bus boycotts begin in Birmingham and Mobile, Alabama, and in Tallahassee, Florida.

Four girls die when the KKK bombs the Sixteenth Street Baptist Church in Birmingham, Alabama.

1954 1955 1956 1957 1960 1961 1963 1965

The Montgomery bus boycott begins on December 5, 1955 and ends on December 21, 1956, when the Supreme Court outlaws segregation in Montgomery.

Fourteen-year-old Emmett Till is murdered in Money, Mississippi, for supposedly whistling at a white woman.

The Little Rock Nine attend Central High School in Little Rock, Arkansas. These students are escorted by federal troops between classes for protection from white students.

Freedom Rides move throughout the southeastern United States.

Freedom Riders are attacked by whites at a bus terminal in Anniston, Alabama.

Martin Luther King Jr. leads a civil rights march from Selma, Alabama, to Montgomery, Alabama.

The Voting Rights Act is passed, putting an end to all methods used by states to keep African Americans from voting.

Little Rock Nine, 1957

Three of the Greensboro Four, 1960

March on Washington, 1963

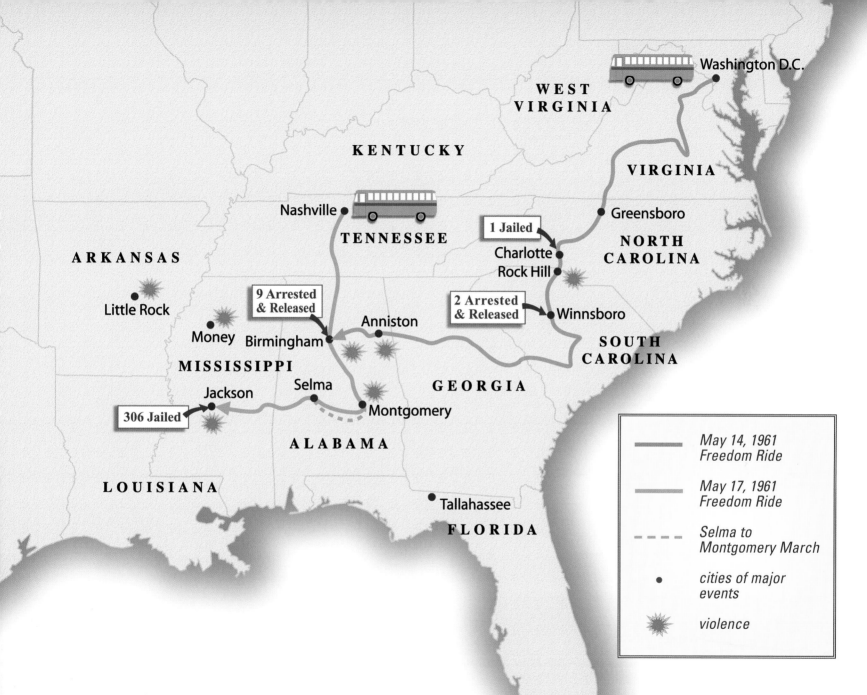

Washington D.C.

WEST VIRGINIA

KENTUCKY

VIRGINIA

Nashville

TENNESSEE

Greensboro

NORTH CAROLINA

1 Jailed

Charlotte
Rock Hill

ARKANSAS

9 Arrested & Released

Anniston

2 Arrested & Released

Winnsboro

SOUTH CAROLINA

Little Rock

Money

Birmingham

GEORGIA

MISSISSIPPI

Jackson

Selma

306 Jailed

Montgomery

ALABAMA

LOUISIANA

Tallahassee

FLORIDA

<table>
<tr><td>———</td><td>May 14, 1961
Freedom Ride</td></tr>
<tr><td>———</td><td>May 17, 1961
Freedom Ride</td></tr>
<tr><td>- - - -</td><td>Selma to
Montgomery March</td></tr>
<tr><td>•</td><td>cities of major
events</td></tr>
<tr><td>✷</td><td>violence</td></tr>
</table>

9

Segregated Schools

In the 1950s, most U.S. schools were segregated. Many people in northern and southern states felt that white children and African American children should not attend the same schools.

In urban areas, African American students attended their own public schools. These schools had indoor plumbing and electricity like schools for white children. But many of the schools were run down and in need of repairs.

In rural areas, African Americans often held classes in abandoned cabins, mule stables, tobacco barns, billiard rooms, and churches. Many rural schools were crude, one-room buildings with shaky floors, cracks in the walls and roofs, and only a potbellied stove for heat. In most cases, the only way for an African American community to build a new building was to close the school for several months and use the teacher's salary to pay for building supplies.

African American schools were in constant risk of being vandalized. Groups such as the KKK sometimes set fire to African American schools. Some families organized secret schools in rural areas to keep students safe. They held classes on different days each week or in different buildings to keep the school a secret.

White children and adults sometimes harassed African American students on their way to school. The sight of African American students carrying books angered whites who did not believe African Americans deserved an education. Children often hid their books in market baskets until they reached the schoolhouse to keep from being harassed.

The NAACP fought for school integration. In the 1950s, the NAACP took a series of cases to the U.S. Supreme Court. These cases were combined in *Brown v. the Board of Education, Topeka*. Linda Brown was a 7-year-old student who lived in Topeka, Kansas. She traveled across town to attend an African American school, even though there was a white school nearby. During the hearing, NAACP attorneys argued that forcing students to attend separate schools because of race made African American children feel bad about themselves.

In 1954, the Supreme Court ruled in favor of the NAACP. The court ruled that even though the school buildings may be equal, separating

Until the 1950s and 1960s, most schools were segregated. The photograph below of Veazy School was taken in 1941.

11

Angry white parents often pulled their children out of newly integrated schools. African American students sat in nearly empty classrooms.

children according to race was harmful to their self-esteem. NAACP attorneys proved that segregation in education had long-lasting effects on children. The courts forced schools to integrate.

Many people still opposed integrated schools. The first African American students to attend white schools often were teased and harassed while on their way to classes. In 1957, nine students tried to attend Central High School in Little Rock, Arkansas. But state officers did not let them into the building. The nine students were Minnijean Brown, Elizabeth Eckford, Ernest Green, Thelma Mothershed, Melba Pattillo, Gloria Ray, Terrence Roberts, Jefferson Thomas, and Carlotta Walls. The U.S. government sent federal troops to protect the students from angry white students and parents. Troops escorted the Little Rock Nine into school and walked with them between classes.

Some African Americans dropped out of white schools because they did not want to be harassed. African American parents sometimes pulled their children out of schools because angry whites threatened the students' lives.

"As they withdrew the troops from inside the corridors, you were subjected to all kinds of taunts, someone attempting to trip you, pour ink on you, in some other way ruin your clothing, and at worst, someone physically attacking you . . . You'd be crazy not to have fear. You kept fear in the back of your mind at all times, a fear that somebody was going to come over and physically harm you, and that nobody would come to your rescue. But we had to be nonviolent. Our nonviolence was an act of logic. We were nine students out of a couple of thousand . . ."
—*Ernest Green, one of the Little Rock Nine, from*
Freedom's Children

Federal troops escorted the Little Rock Nine to class in 1957.

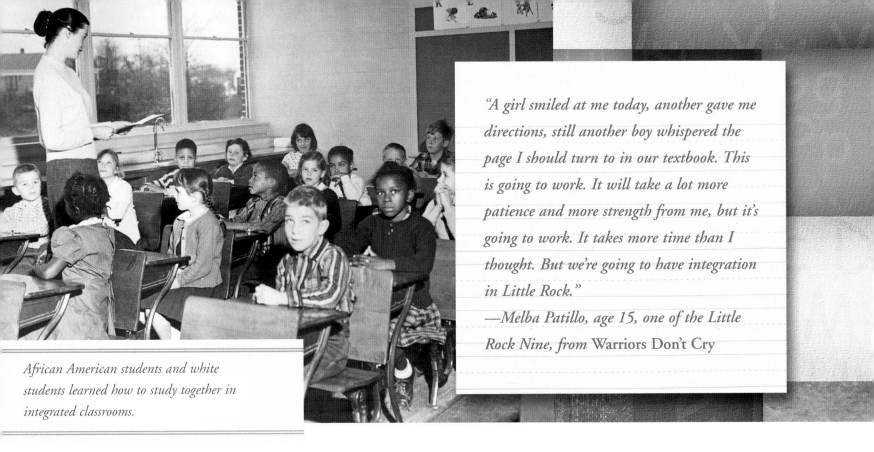

African American students and white students learned how to study together in integrated classrooms.

"A girl smiled at me today, another gave me directions, still another boy whispered the page I should turn to in our textbook. This is going to work. It will take a lot more patience and more strength from me, but it's going to work. It takes more time than I thought. But we're going to have integration in Little Rock."

—Melba Patillo, age 15, one of the Little Rock Nine, from **Warriors Don't Cry**

This result pleased segregationists. They hoped African American parents would not want their children to attend integrated schools. But many African American students remained in integrated schools, so African American students continued to attend.

Many white children were unsure of how to act toward African American students. They were not used to attending racially mixed schools. White students sometimes teased other white classmates for being friends with African American students. Some white children were afraid to include African American students in games or choose them as partners in class projects. They did not want to be harassed. But many white children showed courage by befriending African American students, despite taunts from classmates.

Ruby Bridges

In 1960, 6-year-old Ruby Bridges became the first African American student to attend a desegregated elementary school. A federal court ordered William Frantz Elementary School in New Orleans to allow both African American students and white students to attend. On her first day of classes, many people protested outside the school. Ruby and her mother spent the entire day in the principal's office because of the protesters.

Many parents pulled their children out of school for the entire year. On her second day of school, Ruby thought she was early when she arrived to an empty classroom. Ruby was the only student in her class that year. But she went to school every day. Because of Ruby's courage, more African American children attended William Frantz Elementary School the next year.

A Limited Education

Integration in schools did not come quickly. Many schools remained segregated for several years before federal courts forced them to enroll African American students. Until all public schools were integrated, many African American children continued to attend segregated schools.

In the 1950s, most African American schools taught job skills in addition to basic subjects such as reading, writing, and arithmetic. Schools offered classes in agriculture, cooking, sewing, carpentry, and other trades. Some state policies did not allow African American schools to offer classes in Latin, advanced mathematics, or other subjects that prepared students for college.

African American schools received only a small portion of tax money. Most tax dollars set aside for education went to white schools, even though both African Americans and whites paid taxes. Most African American schools did not have enough money to offer sports activities, drama programs, school libraries, or music programs.

School busing was not always available for African American students. Children often walked several miles to get to school. Other students rode to school on city buses. Segregation laws forced African Americans to ride in the back section of city buses.

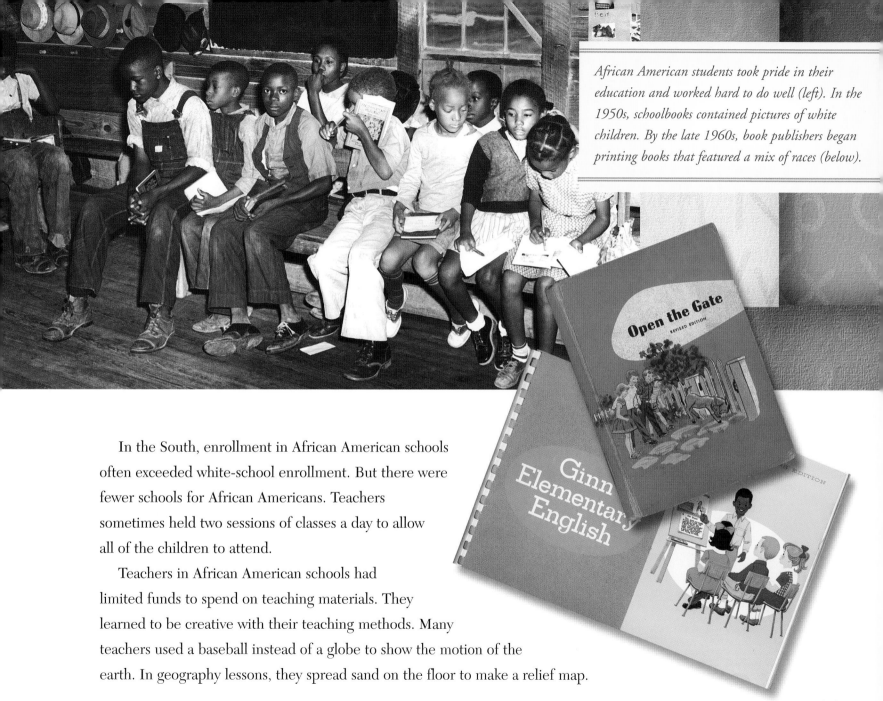

African American students took pride in their education and worked hard to do well (left). In the 1950s, schoolbooks contained pictures of white children. By the late 1960s, book publishers began printing books that featured a mix of races (below).

Open the Gate
REVISED EDITION

Ginn Elementary English

In the South, enrollment in African American schools often exceeded white-school enrollment. But there were fewer schools for African Americans. Teachers sometimes held two sessions of classes a day to allow all of the children to attend.

Teachers in African American schools had limited funds to spend on teaching materials. They learned to be creative with their teaching methods. Many teachers used a baseball instead of a globe to show the motion of the earth. In geography lessons, they spread sand on the floor to make a relief map.

African American schoolteachers had to get by with limited supplies. They used whatever materials they had to give their students a good education.

They formed the sand into mountains, hills, and valleys to show students the landscape in particular areas. With few books in the classroom, many teachers used the Bible and the *Farmer's Almanac* to teach children how to read.

In the 1950s, schools used primers to teach children how to read. Primers taught children a common set of moral and patriotic values. These books included moral tales that promoted faithfulness to employers, respect for authority, cleanliness, and purity. Primers portrayed America as a land of equal opportunity. But African Americans did not have equal opportunities. Primers

Make a Globe

African American schools did not receive as much funding as white schools. Teachers often made their own school supplies. You can make a homemade globe.

What You Need

newspaper

large bowl

dry-ingredient measuring cups

1 cup (250 mL) flour

liquid measuring cup

2 cups (500 mL) water

wooden spoon

styrofoam ball, 6-inch (15-centimeter) diameter, available at craft stores

a map of the world or a globe

green and blue tempera paints

several different-sized paint brushes

styrofoam plate

permanent marker

wooden shish kebab spears

styrofoam disc, 6-inch (15-centimeter) diameter

What You Do

1. Rip several sheets of newspaper into 2-inch (5-centimeter) strips.
2. In a large bowl, combine 1 cup flour (250 mL) and 2 cups (500 mL) water. Stir until well mixed.
3. Dip a strip of newspaper into the flour-water mixture. Make sure the paper is well coated with the mixture.
4. Wrap the paper around the styrofoam ball.
5. Repeat steps 3 and 4 until the ball is completely covered with paper. Let the ball dry overnight.
6. When the ball is dry, paint it blue. Set the ball on a styrofoam plate while painting it. Let the paint dry. Looking at a map or globe, paint the continents onto the ball in green. Let the paint dry. Use the permanent marker to label the continents and oceans.
7. Carefully push the wooden spear into the bottom of the globe. You may need to use two spears to firmly support the globe.
8. Push the other ends of the spears into the styrofoam disc. This disc is the base.

also taught that hard work and honesty brought success. But many employers did not hire or respect African Americans, regardless of their skills or education.

History lessons in primers focused on the superior nature of whites and supported the way whites thought and acted. The books taught about the Pilgrims, the Puritans, and America's Founding Fathers. Books did not include lessons on African American history. Primers often portrayed African Americans as uncivilized, thoughtless, and unintelligent.

In rural areas, African American students crowded into one- or two-room schoolhouses.

Mary McLeod Bethune

Mary McLeod Bethune was born in 1875 in Mayesville, South Carolina. Like many other farm children, Mary worked hard doing chores to help her family. Even when she was very young, she sometimes worked as many as 10 hours a day on the farm.

When Mary was 7 years old, she began attending a mission school in Mayesville, South Carolina. She walked five miles to school each day. After Mary graduated from misson school at age 10, she went to an African American girls boarding school in North Carolina. In order to pay for her room and board, she cleaned and did laundry at the school.

In 1896, Mary began teaching in southern schools. She became a national figure for African American education. In 1904, she opened the Daytona Normal and Industrial Institute for Negro Girls in Florida with only five students. This school eventually became Bethune-Cookman college. Mary served as the school president from 1904 to 1942, and again from 1946 to 1947.

Mary was active in the Civil Rights movement. She served as the director of Negro Affairs of the National Youth Administration and worked with President Franklin Delano Roosevelt on minority issues. She also served as vice president of the NAACP.

A group of students stand around Mary outside Bethune-Cookman College around 1940.

Students as Activists

In the 1950s, many white children spent their free time playing marbles, hopscotch, tag, and kick-the-can. City children played street games with rubber balls. They often lived in tall apartment buildings. These buildings had alleyways between them. The buildings did not have windows on the sides that faced the alleys. Children bounced rubber balls off the walls and tried to catch them. Skilled players would spin around or perform tricks before catching the ball.

In the 1950s and 1960s, many African American children were active in the Civil Rights movement. Instead of playing games with friends, they spent their summers helping civil rights organizations. Some high school students dropped out of school to become full-time civil rights activists. African American children participated in demonstrations, marches, boycotts, and sit-ins. During voter registration drives, they passed out leaflets encouraging people to vote. They also handed out flyers urging people to join boycotts and marches.

Some children helped bring national attention to the Civil Rights movement. In 1951, Barbara Rose Johns demanded improvements at her high school in Farmville, Virginia. Barbara persuaded her classmates to join in a boycott against Morton High School. The NAACP represented her case in court. In 1955 in Montgomery, Alabama, police arrested 15-year-old Claudette Colvin when she refused to give up her seat on a city bus for a white woman. Nine months later, the Montgomery Bus Boycott began to force the city buses to integrate.

During the Montgomery Bus Boycott, children walked to school instead of taking city buses. For some students, this action meant walking many miles across town. African Americans with cars began giving other boycotters rides to school or work. They organized carpools and planned drop-off and pick-up stops throughout the city. The boycott lasted for 382 days, until the U.S. Supreme Court outlawed segregation in Mongomery.

In May of 1963, more than 1,000 students were arrested and jailed for demonstrating against segregation in Birmingham, Alabama. Some of the protesters were only 6 years old. Civil rights leaders asked the children to protest because so many adults already had been jailed. Police unleashed K-9 dog units on the

Students marched to protest segregation. Police sometimes arrested children who participated in demonstrations.

"When the boycott started, I just couldn't wait for morning to come because I wanted to see what was happening. I walked to school. As the buses passed me and my schoolmates, we said, 'Nobody's on the bus! Nobody's on the bus!' It was just a beautiful thing. It was a day to behold to see nobody on the bus."

—Joseph Lacey, age 13, during the Montgomery Bus Boycott, from Freedom's Children

Some people poured salt, ketchup, beverages, or other food on protesters at lunch-counter sit-ins. Some protesters had paint thrown on them or pepper tossed in their eyes.

protesters, and firefighters sprayed them with water from high-pressure fire hoses.

Many young African Americans also particpated in sit-ins. These sit-down protests took place at segregated restaurants and lunch counters. During sit-ins, civil rights activists sat in the white-only sections of segregated areas. Workers refused to serve African Americans who sat in the white section. Activists did not give up their seats when they were asked to move. Many activists were arrested during sit-ins.

Some children were hurt or killed during the Civil Rights movement. In 1955, 14-year-old Emmitt Till was brutally murdered for supposedly whistling at a white woman. The KKK and other groups of angry Southerners bombed homes, schools, churches, and neighborhoods. On September 15, 1963, a bomb set by KKK members killed four African American girls at the Sixteenth Street Baptist Church in Birmingham, Alabama. The victims were 14-year-old Cynthia Wesley, Carole Robertson, and Addie Mae Collins, and 11-year-old Denise McNair.

Study a Sit-in

During the 1950s and 1960s, many civil rights activists participated in sit-ins. In these demonstrations, activists sat in restaurants, theaters, or other public places that allowed only whites to be served. Activists wanted to get the government's attention. They hoped that sit-ins and boycotts would help change laws on segregation. People often harassed activists during sit-ins. Many civil rights activists were beaten or sometimes shot at while participating in sit-ins. Police officers often broke up sit-ins. You can watch footage from actual sit-ins and discuss them with your teacher.

What You Need

"Ain't Scared of Your Jails, 1960-1961," a video of the *Eyes on the Prize* series (available to rent from most public and university libraries and large video stores)

Television
VCR

What You Do

1. Ask your teacher to rent the "Ain't Scared of Your Jails, 1960-1961" video from the *Eyes on the Prize* documentary.
2. Watch the video, paying special attention to the footage of the sit-ins.
3. When the video is over, discuss the footage with your teacher.
4. Talk about how the protesters might have felt when they participated in sit-ins that lasted several hours or all day.
5. Discuss how it was important for protesters to be nonviolent. Discuss how sit-ins helped bring changes in segregation laws.

Celebrations for Strength

During the Civil Rights movement, African Americans found strength in church groups. Members gathered together to give each other comfort and support. In African American churches, members could practice equality. They celebrated victories in the Civil Rights movement. People met at churches to discuss local boycotts, marches, and sit-ins. They shared news and information with each other. At church, African Americans remembered their nonviolence. Leaders such as Reverend Martin Luther King Jr. taught people to be patient and strong. They encouraged civil rights activists to be nonviolent in their fight for equality.

African Americans sang spirituals during church services. They sang these songs to encourage and inspire each other, to stir emotions, and to give the church community a feeling of worth. Most spirituals were based on Biblical stories about people being saved from suffering. The church leader sometimes sang a few lines of the spiritual, and the group responded with the chorus. Spirituals gave people strength to endure hardship during the Civil Rights movement.

During civil rights meetings, marches, and demonstrations, activists sang freedom songs. These songs gave activists encouragement and hope. They sang

Before segregation was outlawed, white children and African American children went to the fair on different days.

songs such as "Freedom Now," "We Shall Overcome," and "Woke Up This Morning with Freedom on My Mind."

African Americans held Freedom Day celebrations. After the Civil War, many African Americans began celebrating Emancipation Day on January 1. On this date in 1801, it became illegal to bring slaves from Africa to the United States. Also, on January 1, 1863, during the Civil War President Abraham Lincoln gave a speech called the Emancipation Proclamation. He declared slaves free in Southern states that were not already under Union control.

Marches and boycotts were special activities. Many people joined together to fight for a common cause. Activists sang freedom songs during marches.

EDMUND PETTUS BRIDGE

In the southwestern United States, people celebrated Emancipation Day on June 19th. On June 19th, 1865, news reached Texas that the Union had won the Civil War and that all slaves were free. African Americans called this celebration Juneteenth.

During Juneteenth, people dressed in fancy clothing. In the mid-1800s, laws regulated slave dress. Slaves were not allowed to wear fancy or expensive clothing. After emancipation, many freed slaves took clothes from plantation owners and tossed their ragged clothes into rivers. Today, Juneteenth is celebrated with parades, carnivals, picnics, and church services. In Washington, D.C., a play about Harriet Tubman and the Underground Railroad is performed on Juneteenth.

Today, U.S. schools honor civil rights leader Martin Luther King Jr. People celebrate Martin Luther King Jr. Day on the third Monday in January. Schools close for this national holiday.

Between 1950 and 1970, the NAACP and workers in the Civil Rights movement brought about many changes in U.S. laws. Many men, women, and children joined together to fight for their rights. Their dedication helped end segregation in schools, transportation, and other public places. Congress also passed many laws to protect the civil rights of all U.S. citizens.

Integrated schools brought students of all races together (above). African American children often attended civil rights meetings in local churches (below).

29

Words to Know

abolish (uh-BOL-ish)—to officially put an end to something

boycott (BOI-kot)—to refuse to use a service as a way of protest

citizenship school (SIT-uh-zuhn-ship SKOOL)—a school that teaches the rights, privileges, and responsibilities of being a U.S. citizen

emancipation (i-MAN-si-pay-shuhn)—freedom from slavery

inferior (in-FIHR-ee-ur)—not equal to another person or thing

integrated (IN-tuh-gray-tid)—combined with more than one race of people

lynch (LINCH)—to put to death by hanging

lynch law (LINCH LAW)—the believed right to kill someone by hanging if accused of a crime instead of giving the person accused a fair trial; the lynch law was not an actual law.

prejudice (PREJ-uh-diss)—an opinion about others that is unfair or not based on facts

protester (PROH-test-ur)—a person who participates in a demonstration against something

rural (RUR-uhl)—an area in the countryside or outside of a city

segregated (SEG-ruh-gay-tid)—separated from something else

sit-in (SIT-in)—to take seats in a racially segregated area as a way of protest; during the Civil Rights movement, sit-ins lasted for several hours or all day.

urban (UR-buhn)—an area in and around a city

vandalized (VAN-duh-lized)—destroyed or damaged by illegal activity

To Learn More

Beals, Melba Pattillo. *Warriors Don't Cry: A Searing Memoir of the Battle to Integrate Little Rock's Central High [Abridged Young Readers Edition]*. New York: Pocket Books, 1995.

Levine, Ellen. *Freedom's Children: Young Civil Rights Activists Tell Their Own Stories*. New York: Putnam, 1993.

Thomas, Velma Maia. *Freedom's Children: The Passage from Emancipation to the Great Migration*. New York: Crown Publishers, 2000.

Turck, Mary C. *The Civil Rights Movement for Kids: A History with 21 Activities*. Chicago: Chicago Review Press, 2000.

Internet Sites

The African American Journey
http://www.worldbook.com/fun/aajourny/html/bh002.html

African American Odyssey
http://lcweb2.loc.gov/ammem/aaohtml/exhibit/aointro.html

African Americans and Formal Education in the American
  South, 1865–1950
http://www.clas.ufl.edu/users/brundage/website/background.html

The Encyclopedia Britannica Guide to Black History
http://www.blackhistory.eb.com

National Civil Rights Museum
http://www.civilrightsmuseum.org

We Shall Overcome: Historic Places of the
  Civil Rights Movement
http://www.cr.nps.gov/nr/travel/civilrights

Places to Visit

Brown v. the Board of Education National Historic Site
424 South Kansas Avenue, Suite 220
Topeka, KS 66603-3441

Little Rock Central High School National Historic Site
2125 West Daisy L. Gatson Bates Drive
Little Rock, AR 72202-5211

Martin Luther King Jr. National Historic Site
450 Auburn Avenue NE
Atlanta, GA 30312-1525

National Civil Rights Museum
450 Mulberry Street
Memphis, TN 38103-4214

Index

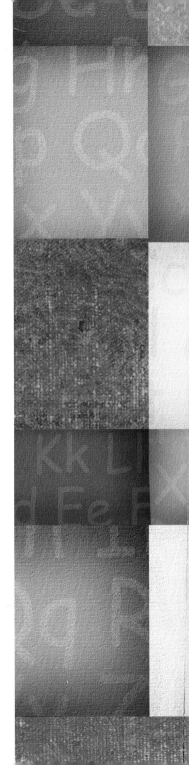